I0521001

THE WAY WITHIN WITHOUT
Recovery Edition

A Modern *Tao Te Ching* Interpretation
For Healing, Presence, and Recovery

Miguel J. Rios

Copyright © 2025 Miguel Rios
All rights reserved.

No part of this publication may be reproduced, distributed, or transmitted in any form or by any means, including photocopying, recording, or other electronic or mechanical methods, without the prior written permission of the author, except in the case of brief quotations embodied in critical reviews and certain other noncommercial uses permitted by copyright law.

For permission requests, write to the author at:

e-Mail: miguel@thewaywithinwithout.com
Website: www.thewaywithinwithout.com

ISBN: 979-8-9936552-1-5

First Edition

Cover design by Miguel J Rios

Published by The Way Within Without Press

To my family:

Who walked The Way beside me
long before I could walk it,
who stayed
when I had no words,
no peace,
and no way out.

Thank you for not giving up.

Praise for *The Way Within Without*

"*The Way Within Without: Recovery Edition* isn't a guide to fixing yourself. It's not a checklist for perfect sobriety or a promise of instant enlightenment. It's something quieter. Slower. Maybe even more honest.

This book is a conversation—between ancient Taoist wisdom and the restless, recovering mind. Between the voice that used to scream for escape and the one learning to whisper, stay.

Across 81 short chapters, Miguel J. Rios offers poetic reflections, recovery-centered meditations, and questions that don't try to solve you so much as invite you back to yourself.

Whether you're newly sober, years into recovery, or simply learning to sit with your own humanity, these verses remind us that healing isn't about becoming someone else. It's about remembering who you've always been beneath the fear and noise.

If you're looking for rules, you won't find them here. What you'll find instead is an invitation—to walk home, one patient step at a time."

— **Eric Zimmer**, host of *The One You Feed*

"At long last, a book for those in recovery that incorporates the generative wisdom of the Tao, the core of gentleness, and the subtlest practices of letting go. Through grounded paradox and ancient poetry, we are invited to be held by centuries of insights, reaching through time to hold us today."

— **Elena Brower**, bestselling author of *Practice You, Being You, Softening Time,* and *Hold Nothing*

"Rios encourages stillness, remembrance, and belonging—helping readers find their way home to themselves."

— **Sharon Salzberg**, author of *Lovingkindness* and *Real Life*

Foreword

Alcohol stole my silence and replaced it with noise.

It numbed my who, what, where, when, why, and how.

For years, I *lived* in fragments: memories *without* meaning, feelings I couldn't name, and pain I thought I had to carry alone. Like many of us who've battled addiction, I became fluent in escaping. I drank to outrun the ache. I drank to drown the noise in my head. I drank to forget the parts of me that had no language yet.

But silence has weight.

Eventually, the bottle doesn't lighten that burden, it only delays the reckoning.

Two years ago, in a Zoom meeting for those in recovery, someone said something that pierced through my autopilot fog. He spoke of mindfulness, not mystically, but with raw simplicity. He said he stayed sober by staying *present*. He would do this by telling himself exactly what he was doing at any given moment, and that would keep him there, in that moment.

That share stopped the noise in my head.

I started reading. Writing. Listening.
I wasn't just searching for sobriety.
I was searching for stillness.
For truth.

For a *way* back to the people and the life I had long abandoned.

That's when I found *The Tao*.

Or it found me.

This book is not a religious text. It's not a set of instructions.

It's a conversation between Lao Tzu, through his words, and the alcoholic in recovery. A dialogue between ancient *Wisdom* and modern chaos, between the voice that once screamed and now whispers.

These verses are a meditation, not a translation.
They're not meant to be analyzed, but absorbed.
They're not rules.
They're reminders.

Reminders of who you are. Of who you've always been:

Beneath the fear.
Beneath the labels.
Beneath the need to fix or be fixed.

Recovery isn't just about quitting drinking.
It's about remembering.
It's about finding *The Way* home.

May this book help you walk home, slowly, honestly, and peacefully.

With love,

—*Miguel J. Rios*

Introduction

The Way Within Without – Recovery Edition is not a translation of the *Tao Te Ching*. It is a modern meditation rooted in *Taoist Wisdom* but filtered through the lived experience of recovery and stillness.

Its eighty-one poetic chapters mirror the rhythm of healing: one day at a time.

Each daily entry offers:

• A poetic verse in the spirit of Taoist wisdom
• A reflection grounded in recovery principles
• Three self-inquiry questions for deeper insight
• A daily affirmation to carry with you

This book is part of a larger whole:

The Book — *The Way Within Without: Recovery Edition* Your daily companion for spiritual grounding and recovery insight.

The Workbook — A space for personal exploration
Includes original book excerpts with **all new journal prompts** for each chapter to help you further reflect upon, write, and internalize the teachings.

The Facilitator's Guide — A path for community practice, offering structure and tools for leading group discussions, making this journey one that can be shared with others in recovery.

Whether you walk this path alone or with others, may it guide you back to what was never truly lost: your inner peace.

—Miguel J. Rios

Author's Note on *The Tao*

The Tao Te Ching was written over 2,500 years ago in China by a man
who walked away from the *Warring States* and a world full of noise.
Lao Tzu didn't preach. He didn't offer rules. He left behind an
understanding of *The Way*, made of paradox and poetry.

That's what makes *The Tao* feel familiar to those of us in recovery:

It doesn't try to fix us. It invites us to return. It reminds us that
healing doesn't have to be loud or perfect.

It can be soft.
It can be slow.
It can begin right now.

I've tried to let the spirit of *The Tao* speak to those in recovery, not as
a scholar, but as someone who drank too much, hurt too deeply, and
finally found a quiet place to land.

May these verses help you soften your grip, slow your breath, and
trust *The Way* going forward.

It's already *Within* you.

— *Miguel J. Rios*

Table of Contents

Day / Chapter 1 – The Hidden Source

The way
you can map
is not The real Way.

The name
you can say
is not the true Name.

What cannot be named
is the Origin
of Heaven and Earth.

What gets named
becomes
mere things and labels.

Let go of wanting,
and glimpse
the mystery.

Hold onto craving,
and you'll see
only the surface.

Mystery and appearance
arise
from the same deep well.

Commentary

In recovery, naming our pain can help us begin to heal, but the source of our suffering often runs deeper than words or 'names.' *The Tao* teaches us that beneath every label: alcoholic, addict, failure, is a more essential mystery: our true nature. To begin recovery is to surrender needing to define ourselves with certainty and instead rest in the mystery. Peace doesn't come from control. It comes from letting go.

Reflection Questions

- What old identities or labels are you ready to let go of?

- How has craving shaped the *way* you see yourself?

- What does it mean to embrace 'not knowing' in your recovery?

Daily Affirmation

Let go of needing to name, label, and define. Peace is in mystery.

Day / Chapter 2 – The Mirror of Opposites

Call something
beautiful,
and ugly
shows up too.

Praise what is
good,
and bad
steps into view.

Being and non-being
make room
for each other.

That is why
the Wise
do not push.

They teach
Without preaching.

They let
things unfold.

They succeed,
Without needing
applause.

Because they do not cling,
nothing
slips away.

Commentary

Recovery means embracing both our darkness and our light.
By resisting shame and comparison, we learn that we don't
need to be perfect: we need to be *present*. When we stop
grasping for praise or hiding in guilt, we make space for
healing.

Reflection Questions

• Where in your *life* do you still label yourself as
'good or bad'?

• Can you allow both your past pain and your
present growth to coexist?

• What would it look like to let go of needing
approval today?

Daily Affirmation

I embrace all that I am, light and shadow alike.

Day / Chapter 3 – The Quiet Leader

*Do not glorify
the clever,
and people
will not compete.*

*Do not prize
possessions,
and theft
will disappear.*

*The Wise
quiet the noise
and raise
stillness.*

*They guide
Without force.*

*They lead
Without pride.*

*And the people remain
content,
clear-minded,
and undisturbed.*

Commentary

In early recovery, we often look to others for answers or try to control every step, but quiet leadership begins *Within*. When we calm the noise of ego and comparison, we start *living* from clarity rather than chaos.

Reflection Questions

- How can you lead yourself with gentleness today?

- What desires or distractions could you release?

- Are you willing to lead through calm rather than control?

Daily Affirmation

Stillness leads me home Without me needing to lead.

Day / Chapter 4 – Bottomless Stillness

The Way
is a bottomless well
—emptied
but never drained.

Silent,
yet the source
of sound.

Present,
yet hidden
in everything.

It blunts sharpness.

Untangles knots.

Softens the glare.

Merges with the dust.

You cannot possess it,
but you can
become it.

It endures
beyond time.

It connects all
Without needing
praise.

Commentary

Addiction can make our world loud, sharp, and tangled, but *The Tao* offers stillness, a quiet *presence* beneath the noise. Recovery invites us to enter this depth, not by force, but by surrender.

Reflection Questions

• Where do you feel most entangled right now?

• How can you soften into stillness rather than fighting the moment?

• What does it feel like to let go of needing to 'fix' yourself or others?

Daily Affirmation

In stillness, I untangle knots and begin again.

Day / Chapter 5 – Impartial Nature

Nature does not take sides
—it nourishes the weeds
and the flowers alike.

The Way
is not sentimental.

It moves
with the rhythm
of what is.

The Wise mirror this way:
open, unattached,
breathing deeply.

They treat all things
like trifling trinkets
—cherished for a time,
then returned
to the soil.

Space gives birth
to breath.

Breath gives birth to form,
but form
must return
to space.

Commentary

Nature has no bias. It creates, destroys, renews, and repeats. When we let go of needing fairness, we begin to see clearly. The skillful treats all things with reverence but knows when to let go.

Reflection Questions

- How do you react when *Life* seems unfair?

- Can you care *Without* clinging?

- What have you been holding on to that is ready to return to the *ground*?

Daily Affirmation

I release what must return to the ground.

Day / Chapter 6 – The Eternal Source

The spirit of the valley
never dies
—it is the womb of
Nature.

This quiet Mother
gives endlessly,
yet never
exhausts herself.

Call it
deep mystery.

Call it
The Root of Life.

Her door
is the Origin
of all.

She whispers
in silence,
forever.

Commentary

The Tao is not a force that demands attention. It is the soft breath behind all creation. Like a mother who nourishes *Without* exhaustion, it sustains *Life* while remaining unseen.

Wisdom means listening to that quiet.

Reflection Questions

- Can you sense the nurturing force behind things?

- Where can you give *Without* depleting yourself?

- How often do you turn toward silence?

Daily Affirmation

In quiet giving, I find purpose and renewal.

Day / Chapter 7 – Staying Behind

Heaven lasts
because it does not
live for itself.

The Earth endures
because it gives
everything away.

The Wise
stand behind,
and find themselves
ahead.

They let go of themselves,
and discover
their true self
intact.

Because they do not
cling,
they cannot
be pushed.

Because they give,
they are
full.

Commentary

Selflessness is not a weakness. It is alignment. The *Wise* remain *grounded* by staying low. In recovery, letting go of ego opens the door to authentic connection between yourself and others. By giving instead of grasping, we become truly whole and develop a sense of community.

Reflection Questions

- Where are you still trying to be ahead or seen first?

- What would it look like to let others go before you today?

- How have you been filled through giving during your recovery?

Daily Affirmation

By giving, I find my true self.

Day / Chapter 8 – Like Water

The highest good
is like water
—nourishing all,
avoiding conflict,
settling in places
where no one chooses.

It dwells
in the low
places.

It flows
in accord
with Nature.

In action—clarity.

In speech—truth.

In ruling—fairness.

In work —ability.

In movement—timing.

It does not compete,
so no one
resents it.

Commentary

Water models recovery, gently, steadily, and humbly. We heal not by rising above others but by *flowing* in harmony with the truth of our *lives*. We find our strength in willingness, not willpower.

Reflection Questions

- Where can you let go of competition and allow *flow*?

- How does humility empower you today?

- What would it mean to move like water in your recovery?

Daily Affirmation

I flow like water: yielding, steady, and soft.

Day / Chapter 9 – Let It Be Full Enough

Better to stop
pouring
than to overflow.

Better to stop
polishing
than to
ruin the shine.

Sharpen a blade
too long,
and it will dull.

Amass too much
wealth,
and you invite
trouble.

Hoard success,
and you guarantee
its loss.

Do your work,
then
let it go.

Commentary

The Tao reminds us that *'enough'* is a powerful word. In addiction, we were never satisfied. In recovery, we learn to stop striving and start *living*. Peace comes when we release the need to prove or perfect.

Reflection Questions

• Where are you overreaching right now?

• What does *'enough'* look like today?

• Can you let go of the outcome after doing your part?

Daily Affirmation

I trust that what I've done is enough for today.

Day / Chapter 10 – Rooted Presence

Can you
hold your soul
and not let it
scatter?

Can you
focus your breath
and become soft
like a newborn?

Can you
cleanse your mind
until it shines
Without stain?

Can you
love people
and lead them
Without control?

Can you
act Without effort,
create Without pride,
give Without claiming?

This is The Rooted presence.

Commentary

Recovery asks us to stay *centered* through chaos. *'The Rooted presence'* means leading from calm, not control, giving *Without* ego, and breathing through discomfort.

Reflection Questions

- When do you feel most scattered, and how can you return to *center*?

- How can you lead your day today *Without* control?

- What does it look like to give freely *Without* pride?

Daily Affirmation

I am Rooted in calm and centered in stillness.

Day / Chapter 11 – The Use of Emptiness

Thirty spokes
join at a hub,
but the center hole
makes the wheel work.

Shape clay
into a pot,
but it is the space inside
that holds what we need.

Cut doors and windows
in a house,
but it is the open space Within
that makes it livable.

We benefit from
what is,
but we live
by what is not.

Commentary

In addiction, we feared emptiness. In recovery, we find it's where healing begins. Space is not lacking. It's a possibility. *The Tao* reminds us that the unseen is just as important as the seen.

Reflection Questions

• What role does stillness play in your *life* today?

• How do you respond to emptiness or silence?

• What spaces in your recovery do you need to protect?

Daily Affirmation

I honor the space that allows healing to unfold.

Day / Chapter 12 – Stay Undistracted

Colors
dazzle the eye.

Sounds
overload the ear.

Flavors
numb the tongue.

Desires
confuse the heart.

Chasing thrills
wastes energy.

The Wise
do not chase.

They return
to the center.

They feed
The Root,
not
the senses.

Commentary

Distraction was a tool we used in addiction. Now, the work is to be *present*. *The Tao* reminds us to feed *The Root*, not the noise. Returning to the *center* is how we stay *grounded* when *Life* spins out of control.

Reflection Questions

- What distractions are pulling you from your purpose today?

- What does it mean to *'feed The Root'* in recovery?

- How can you practice choosing stillness over stimulation?

Daily Affirmation

I return to The Root and release the noise.

Day / Chapter 13 – Let Go of Status

Favor and disgrace
both
unsettle.

Status and self
are
illusions.

Why is favor
unsettling?

Because we fear
losing it.

Why is disgrace
unsettling?

Because we cling
to our image.

Drop the need to be
someone,
and nothing
can disturb you.

Care for the world
as you care
for your body
—not because of glory,
but because of presence.

Commentary

In addiction, we often tried to be someone important, liked, or validated. In recovery, we let go of those masks. *The Tao* teaches that peace doesn't come from status but from *presence*. What matters is not who we appear to be but who we truly are.

Reflection Questions

• How much of your self-worth still depends on 'others' approval?

• What does it mean to drop your image and *live* in *presence*?

• How can you show up today *Without* needing to be seen?

Daily Affirmation

I let go of image and live from the essence of presence.

Day / Chapter 14 – Beyond Sight

Look
—there is nothing
to see.

Listen
—there is nothing
to hear.

Reach
—there is nothing
to grasp.

The Way cannot be sensed
—yet it is always
with you.

It rises
from nowhere,
and returns
to nowhere.

It has
no name,
yet it holds
every name.

Follow it,
and you follow
your deep
nature.

Commentary

Recovery is not always visible. Our progress can't always be measured by what others see. Like *The Tao*, transformation often happens quietly, invisibly, and inwardly. Trust what is working beneath the surface.

Reflection Questions

- Where in your *life* are you looking for results instead of trusting?

- What unseen support carries you right now?

- Can you follow your inner *path* even if it feels unclear?

Daily Affirmation

I trust The unseen Way that leads me inward.

Day / Chapter 15 – The Way of the Skillful

The Wise ancients
moved in silence
—watchful and alert:

careful like crossing
a frozen stream,
gentle like a guest,
open like melting snow,
steady like a mountain,
clear like a mirror.

They did not
chase answers.

They waited for
clarity.

They did not
impose.

They
responded.

Rooted
in The Way,
they left
no trace.

Commentary

The skillful in recovery don't rush. They pause, breathe, and move gently. Like crossing ice, they are mindful of each step. We don't need to force answers. We can wait for clarity.

Reflection Questions

- How can you move more gently through today?

- Are you rushing for clarity instead of waiting for it?

- What would it mean to leave no trace of ego behind you?

Daily Affirmation

I move gently, guided by the quiet strength of presence.

Day / Chapter 16: The Still Point

Quiet
the mind
—and the world
stills.

In stillness,
the dust
begins to
settle.

All things rise
and fall,
but the Source
remains.

To return to it
is to find
rest
—Rooted
in the
unchanging.

Those who
remember The Root
flow through change
Without losing
themselves.

Commentary

This chapter speaks to the essence of recovery, returning to a more profound stillness *Within*. When we stop chasing every thought, urge, or fear, we begin to reconnect with something constant and enduring. *The Tao* is that steady *presence* underneath the storm. By learning to sit in stillness, we return to our true selves, and the compulsion to escape fades. In recovery, silence isn't empty. It's a healing force.

Reflection Questions

- When was the last time you honestly sat in silence *Without* distraction?

- What part of you feels most *Rooted* in stillness?

- How can you begin to trust quiet more than chaos?

Daily Affirmation

I return to The Root and find peace.

Day / Chapter 17: The Invisible Way

*The best
leaders
are barely
known.*

*Next best
are
loved.*

*Then,
feared.*

*Then,
despised.*

*If you don't
trust people,
they become
untrustworthy.*

*The Wise
speak
little.*

*When their tasks
are done,
the people
say,*

'We did it ourselves.'

Commentary

In recovery, we learn that the most profound changes often occur quietly. There is no fanfare, no forcing, just *presence* and trust. This applies to how we lead others and how we lead ourselves. We stop trying to control everything. Instead, we listen, offer gentle support, and allow growth to occur naturally. Trusting the process is *The* invisible *Tao.*

Reflection Questions

• What kind of inner leader do you follow?

• Where in your *life* are you trying too hard to be seen or acknowledged?

• How does trust change your relationship with others and yourself?

Daily Affirmation

I trust quiet leadership.

Day / Chapter 18: Losing the Way

When
The Way
is lost,
morality appears.

When
love fades,
duty takes its place.

When
harmony breaks,
rules multiply.

When
truth is absent,
loyalty is enforced.

This
leads to
chaos.

Commentary

This verse exposes how we drift from authenticity. In addiction, we often overcompensate with rigid morals, rules, or personas, trying to cover the inner loss. Recovery brings us back to *The Root*, where love *flows* naturally, and truth doesn't need enforcement. When we *live* from *The Tao*, we no longer need to pretend or perform.

Reflection Questions

- Have you ever used 'doing the right thing' to mask pain or fear?

- What happens when you try to force love or honesty?

- How does returning to your inner truth restore your outer *life*?

Daily Affirmation

I choose authenticity over appearance.

Day / Chapter 19: Empty Your Mind

Drop
wisdom.

Let go
of morality.

Forget
cleverness.

Return
to The Root.

Give up striving
—and return to
simplicity.

Release the rules
—and return to
what's real.

A quiet mind
needs
no map.

Commentary

Letting go of 'should have, could have, and would have' is the cornerstone of recovery. We are invited to return to simplicity, *presence*, and what is real. Cleverness, striving, and rigid ideas often kept us stuck. Now, we make room for clarity by releasing the clutter. When we empty the mind, we create space for grace to *flow* in.

Reflection Questions

• What mental clutter are you ready to release?

• What does simplicity look like for you today?

• How can you return to what's real *Without* needing to 'figure it all out'?

Daily Affirmation

I release the noise and return to simplicity.

Day / Chapter 20: Different Path

Give up
what others chase.

Stop
comparing.

The masses
rush and strive
—I move
slowly.

They are excited
—I am
still.

They know so much
—I remain
empty.

I am different
—and at peace
with that.

Commentary

Recovery is a different *path*. While the world rushes, we slow down. While others chase highs or achievements, we pursue *presence*. This chapter affirms the courage it takes to walk a quieter, serene *way*. We stop comparing and begin accepting our unique rhythm. That is where peace *lives*.

Reflection Questions

• Where do you feel pressured to keep up with others?

• How does your recovery *path* look different, and why is that okay?

• What helps you stay *grounded* in your own pace?

Daily Affirmation

I walk my own path, in peace.

Day / Chapter 21: The Formless Flow

The greatest
presence
is invisible.

It moves through
all things,
yet clings
to none.

Vague and shifting,
it holds the shape
of every form
Without becoming
one.

This is The Way
of The Way
—shadow of substance,
The Root of all being.

Commentary

The Tao cannot be grasped, yet it touches everything. Recovery reminds us that the most potent forces in our *lives*: love, grace, and spirit often come unseen. *The Tao* is the undercurrent that carries us when we stop trying to control the tide. Our task is not to force *life* but to *flow* with it.

Reflection Questions

• Where have you felt a quiet force guiding you in recovery?

• What happens when you stop trying to force a solution?

• How can you practice *flowing* with *Life* rather than resisting it?

Daily Affirmation

I trust the unseen flow of The Way.

Day / Chapter 22: Wholeness in Yielding

Bend
to be whole.

Empty
to be filled.

Break
to be renewed.

Let go
to be held.

The soft
overcomes the hard.

The humble
outlasts the proud.

This is the paradox
of The Way.

Commentary

In recovery, strength comes through surrender. What once broke us becomes the doorway to healing. When we yield instead of resisting, *The Tao* restores us. We learn that humility is not weakness, it is a state of alignment. Softness opens us to grace. Surrender makes room for wholeness.

Reflection Questions

• Where has surrender brought you strength?

• What part of you needs softening today?

• How can you bend instead of break in your journey?

Daily Affirmation

I surrender to become whole.

Day / Chapter 23: Fewer Words, Deeper Truth

Nature doesn't
speak
—yet everything
gets done.

A whirlwind
doesn't last long.

A storm
settles itself.

Those in harmony
with The Way
speak little,
act with clarity,
and trust
the rest to unfold.

Commentary

In early recovery, we may feel the need to explain ourselves, justify our actions, and speak constantly. Still, as we delve deeper, we realize that the truth doesn't require many words. *The Tao* teaches us to quiet ourselves and be *present*. Simplicity and *presence* speak for themselves.

Reflection Questions

• Where can you speak less and listen more?

• How do your actions reflect your inner truth?

• What would change if you stopped trying to prove yourself?

Daily Affirmation

My presence speaks louder than my words.

Day / Chapter 24: The Root of Pride

Stand on tiptoe,
and you wobble.

Rush ahead,
and you trip.

Show off,
and you lose respect.

Exaggerate,
and you become hollow.

The Way needs
no display.

It flows
low,
steady,
unseen.

Commentary

Ego once fueled our addiction by always needing to be seen, to be right, to be in control. Recovery invites us to step down from the pedestal and walk humbly. Pride makes us unstable, but when we let go of image and ambition, we begin to walk a steadier *Tao*.

Reflection Questions

- Where is pride creating an imbalance in your recovery?

- How do you feel when you let go of the need to impress?

- What would it mean to walk humbly today?

Daily Affirmation

I choose humility over pride.

Day / Chapter 25: That Which Cannot Be Named

There is something
vast and formless
—older than
Heaven and Earth.

Silent.

Empty.

Alone.

It never
changes.

It moves in circles,
flows through all things.

We call it
The Way.

It gives birth to all,
nourishes all,
guides all,
Without needing to control.

Commentary

This mysterious force, *The Tao*, does not demand worship, only awareness. In recovery, we may struggle with the word 'God,' but what we're truly seeking is not a name but a *presence*. We don't need to define it. We need to only remember it.

Reflection Questions

- What does the word *'Tao'* mean to you personally?

- How does it feel to connect with something nameless and vast?

- What happens when you let go of needing to control everything?

Daily Affirmation

I walk with The nameless Way.

Day / Chapter 26: Weight of Stillness

The heavy
is The Root
of the light.

Stillness
is the expert
of motion.

The Wise
stay grounded
—even in a storm.

Surrounded by noise,
they carry stillness
like a
precious stone.

Commentary

In recovery, stillness becomes our anchor. While the world moves frantically, we choose to *ground* ourselves. Stillness doesn't mean inaction. It implies *presence*. When chaos rises, we don't chase it or run from it. We return to our breath, our truth, our weight. It's this *Rootedness* that keeps us sober.

Reflection Questions

• What *grounds* you when *Life* feels unsteady?

• Where do you need more stillness today?

• How can you carry inner weight instead of chasing external noise?

Daily Affirmation

I carry stillness like a sacred stone.

Day / Chapter 27: The Skillful Step

A good traveler
leaves
no trail.

A Wise speaker
needs
no correction.

A skilled healer
needs
no praise.

The Wise
live simply
—and leave
nothing
broken.

Commentary

Recovery humbles us. We often learn that the most significant impact can go unnoticed. The ego seeks credit, but healing seeks *presence*. We don't need to announce our growth. It shows. Just as *The Tao* leaves no trace but shapes all things, we begin to *live* with gentle *Wisdom*, doing good quietly.

Reflection Questions

- Where are you seeking recognition instead of peace?

- What does humility look like in action for you?

- Can you let your healing speak *Without* words?

Daily Affirmation

I walk gently and leave no trace.

Day / Chapter 28: Embrace Both

*Know
the masculine,
but stay with
the feminine.*

*Be the riverbed
—soft and low.*

*Hold strength
Without
hardness.*

*Be whole
—by
embracing both.*

Commentary

We are all a balance of opposites: light and shadow, strength, and softness. Recovery teaches us not to over-identify with roles, but to integrate them. A real strength is flexibility. Real tenderness is resilience. *The Tao* invites us to hold the tension gently, becoming whole through balance.

Reflection Questions

• Where do you resist your softer or firmer side?

• How does integration feel different from perfection?

• What parts of yourself are ready to be welcomed home?

Daily Affirmation

I am whole by embracing both sides.

Day / Chapter 29: Let Things Unfold

*Do you want
to rule
the world?*

Don't.

*It's a precious
vessel
—you'll only
break it.*

*Some things
must not
be forced.*

*Try to
control,
and you
destroy.*

*Let go,
and
The Way
flows.*

Commentary

Recovery reminds us that control is an illusion. When we tried to manage everything, we only deepened our suffering. But letting go doesn't mean apathy. It means trust. Trust that *The Tao* has its own rhythm. Our job isn't to fix the world. It's to stop breaking ourselves.

Reflection Questions

• Where are you trying to force *Life* to fit your plan?

• What would it look like to truly let go today?

• How does trust change your experience of the unknown?

Daily Affirmation

I let go and trust in the unfolding.

Day / Chapter 30: Beyond Aggression

Those who conquer
by force
invite
their own fall.

The strongest Way
is
gentleness.

True power
does not need
to harm.

Tread lightly
—stay close
to the ground.

Commentary

In addiction, we often use force on others or on ourselves. Recovery shows us a better *way*: gentleness. Lasting change doesn't come through punishment but through compassion. *The Tao* does not fight, yet nothing resists it. In our healing, we stop pushing and start softening.

Reflection Questions

• How has aggression shown up in your recovery journey?

• What does gentle strength feel like inside you?

• How can you lead with softness today?

Daily Affirmation

My strength is found in gentleness.

Day / Chapter 31: Weapons Are not the Way

Weapons are
tools of fear.

They are not
The Way
of the Wise.

Even in victory,
there is no
celebration.

The Way
mourns
when blood is
spilled.

The Way walks
Without
violence.

Commentary

Violence isn't just physical, it's in the words we hurl at others, the pressure we put on ourselves, and the anger we cling to. Recovery invites a gentler *way*. Winning doesn't mean overpowering. It means choosing peace. We learn to walk away from battles, especially those *Within* ourselves.

Reflection Questions

- Where are you still fighting, inside or outside of yourself?

- How do you respond when you feel threatened or afraid?

- What would it mean to choose peace today?

Daily Affirmation

I lay down the weapons of fear.

Day / Chapter 32: The Nameless Stream

The Way
is
forever nameless.

Like a stream
flowing
through the world
—it nourishes
all
Without control.

Name it,
and it
becomes
a doctrine.

Leave it unnamed,
and it
flows
free.

Commentary

The Tao doesn't need control. It *flows* on its own. In early recovery, structure helps us find footing, but as we grow, we're called to release even the need to manage *The Tao*. Just like a river gathers many streams, *The Tao* welcomes many forms. What matters isn't the method. It's staying close to what's simple, natural, and true. Let *The Tao* carry you.

Reflection Questions

• What labels are you ready to release?

• How does it feel to *live Without* needing to define everything?

• Where are you invited to *flow* freely today?

Daily Affirmation

I flow beyond all names.

Day / Chapter 33: True Strength

Knowing others
is intelligence.

Knowing yourself
is Wisdom.

Mastering others
is force.

Mastering yourself
is true power.

Those who stay
content
are truly rich.

Those who endure
have lasting will.

This is the strength
of those
who do not
struggle.

Commentary

Addiction had power over us. Recovery taught us to reclaim it, not by controlling others, but by understanding ourselves. This is the heart of *The Tao:* inner mastery. Self-awareness, self-kindness, and patience are real power moves. We stop trying to fix others and begin to know ourselves.

Reflection Questions

• What is one thing you now understand about yourself that you didn't before recovery?

• Where are you still trying to master others instead of yourself?

• What does true inner strength look like for you?

Daily Affirmation

My power is in knowing myself.

Day / Chapter 34: The Ocean Beneath All

The Way
flows
everywhere.

It nourishes
all things
—yet asks
for nothing.

It holds
all,
and possesses
none.

So small,
it fits
in every heart.

So vast,
it contains
the stars.

Commentary

The Tao, like recovery, is a quiet gift. It supports us *Without* demanding repayment. We begin to feel its *presence* when we slow down, breathe, and open up. It doesn't control us. It frees us. The more we trust this quiet ocean, the more peace we find *Within* ourselves.

Reflection Questions

- When have you felt quietly supported by *Life* itself?

- How does it feel to receive *Without* needing to earn it?

- Where is *The Tao* moving gently in your *life* today?

Daily Affirmation

I am held by something vast and gentle.

Day / Chapter 35: The Quiet Magnet

Hold to the
Great Image
—and the world
will come.

People come
not for words,
but for the quiet
pull of truth.

The Way
is calm
—but nourishes
all things.

Commentary

You don't have to chase anyone or anything. In recovery, we learn that authenticity attracts what is meant for us. We stop selling ourselves or shouting to be heard. *The Tao* is like a quiet magnet: its power is stillness. You don't need to persuade. Just be true. That's *enough.*

Reflection Questions

- Where are you chasing what you could be attracting?

- What does it mean to *live* in quiet truth?

- How can you *Root* deeper into authenticity today?

Daily Affirmation

I attract by being fully present.

Day / Chapter 36: Pull Back to Move Forward

If you want
to shrink something,
first let it
expand.

If you want
to weaken something,
first allow it
to grow strong.

If you want to take,
first give.

This is subtle
Wisdom
—softening
before
redirecting.

Commentary

The Tao teaches through paradox. In recovery, we sometimes must sit with discomfort, allow space, or even release control before change can happen. We don't force healing. We make room for it. Real progress often appears as a pause, a breath, or a moment of pulling back before moving forward.

Reflection Questions

• Where in your *life* are you forcing change too quickly?

• How might softening or stepping back open a *way* forward?

• What would it feel like to trust the pause?

Daily Affirmation

I step back to move forward.

Day / Chapter 37: Do Less, Become More

The Way
does nothing,
yet leaves
nothing undone.

If leaders
aligned with it,
all things
would unfold
Without force.

Stillness
 leads
—not
striving.

Commentary

Striving once drove us to exhaustion. In recovery, we learn the opposite: less can be more. *The Tao* reminds us that we don't need to force healing. It arises naturally when we are *present*. *The Tao* leads through stillness, not stress. We do less, and *Life* begins to move.

Reflection Questions

- Where are you still trying to earn your worth through effort?

- What part of your healing could benefit from more stillness?

- What does doing less look like in your recovery today?

Daily Affirmation

I allow by being, not by forcing.

Day / Chapter 38: False Virtue

True virtue
does not try
to be virtuous.

Those who try
to be good
are not
truly good.

The Wise
act
Without show.

They love
Without
needing praise.

When
The Way
is lost,
codes and morals
arise.

Commentary

Recovery teaches us to stop performing. When we lose touch with *The Tao*, we start playing roles, trying to look good instead of being real, but true integrity doesn't advertise itself. We show up humbly and honestly. There's nothing to prove. Walk *The Tao*.

Reflection Questions

• Where are you performing instead of being true?

• What happens when you stop trying to be 'good' and start being real?

• How can you return to an authentic *presence* today?

Daily Affirmation

I release the show and return to truth.

Day / Chapter 39: The One

Heaven is clear
because of
The One.

Earth is steady
because of
The One.

All things
arise from it
—and return
to it.

To forget
The One
is to
fall.

To honor
The One
is to be
whole.

Commentary

The Tao is *The One*: *source, presence, and flow.* In recovery, we often reconnect with this profound sense of unity. Whether we call it God, a Higher Power, Truth, or *Tao*, we recognize something larger that holds us. Honoring that connection keeps us *grounded*, humble, and aligned with *Life*.

Reflection Questions

• What does *'The One'* mean to you in your recovery?

• When do you feel most connected to something greater?

• How can you return to that unity today?

Daily Affirmation

I live in harmony with The One.

Day / Chapter 40: Return and Yielding

Return
is the movement
of The Way.

Yielding
is the movement
of strength.

All things
arise
from being.

Being
emerges
from non-being.

Commentary

Taoist *Wisdom* often returns to these two truths: we must return, and we must yield. In recovery, we return to *presence*, to ourselves, and to honesty. And we yield, no longer forcing, fighting, or numbing. This is strength. This is surrender. This is *The Tao*.

Reflection Questions

- What do you need to return to today?

- Where are you being invited to yield instead of push?

- How does surrender feel like strength in your journey?

Daily Affirmation

In returning and yielding, I find my strength.

Day / Chapter 41: The Way Seems Backward

When the highest seekers
hear of The Way,
they follow
it with devotion.

When average seekers
hear of The Way,
they question
and debate.

When shallow seekers
hear of The Way,
they laugh.

And that's how
you know it's
The Way.

The Way
moves
opposite of
what the world
expects.

Commentary

Recovery often feels backward to the outside world. We slow down instead of speeding up. We surrender instead of controlling. But this is what makes it powerful. Genuine seekers recognize that *The Tao* isn't flashy. It's quiet, slow, and looks inward. Keep walking, even if others don't understand.

Reflection Questions

• What parts of your *path* feel misunderstood by others?

• How do you stay faithful to your truth even when it's questioned?

• Where has the 'backward' *path* led you to healing?

Daily Affirmation

I trust The quiet Way, even when it feels backwards.

Day / Chapter 42: The Birth of All Things

The Way
gives birth
to One.

One
gives birth
to Two.

Two
gives birth
to Three.

Three
gives birth
to Nature.

Nature carries
Yin
and embraces
Yang
—held together
in the breath
of harmony.

Commentary

Everything begins in stillness and then unfolds into form. In recovery, we reconnect with this cycle of creation in spirit, awareness, and balance. *Yin and Yang* remind us that we are not broken, but we are both shadows and light. Embracing both brings wholeness.

Reflection Questions

- Where do you see light and shadow coexisting in your *life*?

- How does understanding your non-dual nature bring healing?

- What part of you is being reborn today?

Daily Affirmation

I am both light and shadow, held in harmony.

Day / Chapter 43: Soft Overcomes Hard

The softest thing
in the world
outlasts
the hardest.

Water
carves through
stone.

Silence
breaks through
noise.

In this,
we see
The Way
of The Way
—gentle,
yet
unstoppable.

Commentary

You don't need to push to create change. In recovery, the gentlest acts: saying no, being *present*, and breathing, become your greatest strengths. Softness is not weakness. It's *Wisdom*. Water doesn't have to rage, but it can shape canyons over time. Walk gently, and you will move mountains.

Reflection Questions

- What would it look like to move through your day with softness?

- Where in your *life* can gentle *presence* be effective?

- How does softness bring real power into your healing?

Daily Affirmation

I overcome by yielding, not by force.

Day / Chapter 44: Letting Go Wins

Fame or integrity
—which
matters
more?

Money or wholeness
—which is
worth
more?

Gain or loss
—which
brings more
pain?

The one
who clings
loses.

The one
who lets go
is free.

Commentary

In addiction, we cling to what we are never satisfied with. Recovery asks us to loosen our grip on success, appearance, and fear. When we let go, we open up. True freedom doesn't come from getting more. It comes from needing less. Let go and receive what lasts.

Reflection Questions

- What are you holding on to that's holding you back?

- Where can you choose integrity over image today?

- What would it feel like to let go, just a little?

Daily Affirmation

I let go, and in letting go, I am free.

Day / Chapter 45: Wholeness in Imperfection

True completeness
may seem
incomplete
—yet it never
fails.

True fullness
may seem
empty
—yet it never
runs dry.

Stillness
appears
slow.

Clarity
appears
dull.

The Way
hides
in the
ordinary.

Commentary

You don't have to be impressive to be whole. In recovery, we begin to embrace our imperfections. *The Tao* doesn't seek perfection. It seeks *presence*. You are already *enough*. Healing isn't flashy. It's subtle, quiet, and serene. Trust what seems incomplete.

Reflection Questions

- Where have you mistaken wholeness for perfection?

- How does it feel to be *enough Without* needing to prove it?

- What small, quiet parts of you carry profound *Wisdom?*

Daily Affirmation

I am whole, even in my imperfection.

Day / Chapter 46: Contentment Is Power

When the world
follows
The Way,
horses work
in fields.

When the world
forgets
The Way,
warhorses are trained
instead.

There is no
greater loss
than never
being satisfied.

There is no
greater wealth
than
contentment.

Commentary

Recovery gives us something that addiction never could: *enough*. When we were caught in the spiral, nothing satisfied us. Now, we learn to savor stillness, *presence*, and peace. Contentment is not settling. It's freedom from craving. The more we stop chasing, the more we arrive.

Reflection Questions

• What does contentment feel like in your body and heart?

• Where are you still searching outside for something only found *Within* you?

• How can you nurture gratitude for what already is?

Daily Affirmation

I have enough. I am enough.

Day / Chapter 47: The Inner World

Without
leaving
your home,
you can
know
the world.

Without
looking out
the window,
you can
see
The Way.

The farther
you go,
the less
you
understand.

The Wise
look
Within.

Commentary

Recovery turns our attention inward. While we once sought answers outside, in people, places, and things, we now learn to listen *Within*. *The Tao* is not out there. It's here in our, breath, body, and *presence*. When we stop running, we find we've always had what we needed.

Reflection Questions

• Where are you still seeking outward instead of *Within*?

• What happens when you get quiet and listen inside?

• What inner truth have you been avoiding, but you are now ready to face?

Daily Affirmation

I find truth by turning Within.

Day / Chapter 48: Letting Go of Knowing

*In pursuit of
knowledge,
we add more
each day.*

*In pursuit of
The Way,
we let go
each day.*

*Less and less
—until nothing
is left.*

*And nothing
is
undone.*

Commentary

Letting go is *The Tao*. In recovery, we learn to release our need to figure everything out. We stop trying to control the future or explain the past. *The Tao* doesn't demand knowledge. It invites *presence*. Less doing, less knowing, more being. That's *The Tao*.

Reflection Questions

• What belief or thought can you release today?

• Where is your 'need to know' creating tension?

• How would it feel to trust instead of analyzing?

Daily Affirmation

I release knowing and rest in being. The doing of non-doing.

Day / Chapter 49: The Heart That Holds All

The Wise
have no fixed
heart
—they hold
the hearts
of all.

They are
kind
to the kind,
and kind
to the unkind
—because
kindness
is their nature.

They listen
to the world,
and the world
listens back.

Commentary

Judgments kept us sick. In recovery, we find freedom through compassion. We don't condone harm, but we hold space for healing. The *Wise* aren't reactive, they're receptive. When we lead with kindness, even when it's hard, we soften our suffering.

Reflection Questions

- Where are you still holding resentment?

- How can compassion help you release it?

- What would it mean to *'hold the hearts of all'* gently?

Daily Affirmation

I lead with a heart that holds all.

Day / Chapter 50: Choose Life

Some walk
The Path
of Life.

Others
cling to
death.

They chase
danger,
cut themselves down,
and call it
living.

But those who live
in The Way
walk through
the valley
unharmed.

They choose
peace
—and peace
walks with
them.

Commentary

Addiction pulls us toward death, slowly or suddenly. Recovery is a choice to live. Not just survive but truly live. *The Tao* protects those who walk with *presence*. We don't tempt fate anymore.

Reflection Questions

- What does choosing *Life* mean to you today?

- Where are you still entertaining self-harm in subtle ways?

- How can you honor your *life* with gentleness and care?

Daily Affirmation

I choose Life, and Life chooses me.

Day / Chapter 51: The Way Gives Life

*The Way
gives Life to
Nature.*

*Virtue
nourishes
it.*

*Form
shapes
it.*

*Circumstances
complete
it.*

*Nature honors
The Way
—not by
command,
but by
being alive.*

*The Way
gives,
and does not
take
credit.*

Commentary

The Tao sustains us with quiet generosity. In recovery, we begin to sense this subtle gift, the breath that continues and the light that returns. We don't need to force *Life* into meaning. It's already full of grace.

Reflection Questions

- Where do you sense *The Tao* sustaining your recovery?

- What does it feel like to receive *Without* earning?

- How can you honor the *Life Within* you today?

Daily Affirmation

I receive Life from The Way, Without needing to earn it.

Day / Chapter 52: Return to The Mother

The Way
is
the Mother
of
the world.

Know
the Mother,
and
you know
her children.

Guard the Mother,
and you'll never
stray.

Open your heart
to light,
but stay
Rooted
in the dark.

Be a valley
—empty,
deep,
receptive.

Commentary

We return to the *Source* not through striving but through softening. In recovery, the dark no longer scares us, we know it's *The Root* of all growth. *The Tao* is like a *mother*: still, loving, and firm. When we dwell in her *presence*, we are safe. Keep coming home to *Mother*.

Reflection Questions

- What does it mean for you to *'return to the Mother'*?

- How do you stay *Rooted* in depth while walking toward light?

- Where are you being called to soften and receive?

Daily Affirmation

I return to the Source and find rest.

Day / Chapter 53: Stay on The Path

If I have
even a little
Wisdom,
I walk the
Great Path
—and fear
only straying.

The Way
is smooth
and straight
—yet people
prefer shortcuts.

Their palaces
are grand,
but their fields
are bare.

They wear
fine clothes,
but carry
hidden shame.

This is
not
The Way.

Commentary

In recovery, we're tempted to look for shortcuts, quick fixes, bypasses, and false pride. But *The Tao* is simple, and simplicity requires honesty. Don't rush. Stay real. *The Tao* is already here. The work is walking it.

Reflection Questions

- Where are you tempted to shortcut your healing?

- What does it look like to walk *The Tao* today?

- How does honesty keep you aligned with *The Tao*?

Daily Affirmation

I stay with The Way: simple, steady, true.

Day / Chapter 54: Root Deep, Rise Steady

What is well
Rooted
cannot be
uprooted.

What is well
held
cannot slip
away.

Your life
becomes real,
then
your family,
your town,
your country,
the world.

The Way
begins Within
—and grows
Without.

Commentary

Recovery *Roots* us. First in ourselves, then in relationships, and then in community. If the foundation is deep, the growth is steady. Don't worry about fixing everything outside. Start with your *center*. What you tend to will ripple outward in time.

Reflection Questions

• How are you tending to your inner *roots* today?

• What keeps you *grounded* when storms come?

• Where do you see your healing impacting others?

Daily Affirmation

I Root deep, so I may rise steady.

Day / Chapter 55: Return to Innocence

Those who live
in harmony
with
The Way
are like
newborns.

Soft bones.

Gentle hearts.

They cry
with power
—yet no harm
comes to
them.

They
walk
unafraid.

To live long
—stay close
to
innocence.

To force Life
—is to lose
Life.

Commentary

Addiction hardened us. Recovery softens us again. Like children, we learn to feel *Without* shame, speak *Without* armor, and walk *Without* fear. *The Tao* invites us not to grow up, but to grow back into who we were before the pain. That's innocence. That's peace.

Reflection Questions

• What part of your innocence is returning?

• How do you protect your softness *Without* closing your heart?

• Where can you let yourself be vulnerable today?

Daily Affirmation

I return to innocence and walk Without fear.

Day / Chapter 56: Those Who Know Don't Speak

*Those who
know
do not
speak.*

*Those who
speak
do not
know.*

*Close your
mouth.*

*Quiet your
mind.*

Be still.

Be open.

*This is
The Way.*

Clarity.

Commentary

Recovery teaches us the power of silence. When we were loud, we were often hiding. Now, we learn that truth doesn't always need to be said. It's *lived*. We speak less, listen more, and let *presence* do the work. Stillness becomes a teacher.

Reflection Questions

- Where in your *life* can you practice more silence?

- How has stillness helped you hear what truly matters?

- What would it feel like 'to be,' *Without* explaining yourself?

Daily Affirmation

I know and become through stillness, not speech.

Day / Chapter 57: Lead Without Force

*Use fairness
to lead a
country.*

*Use surprise
to lead an
army.*

*Use non-interference
to lead a
life.*

*The more rules
you make,
the more
malcontents
appear.*

*The Wise
lead
Without
controlling.*

*They teach
by
being.*

Commentary

In recovery, we stop trying to control others or ourselves. We lead our *lives* gently, not with rules or fear, but with quiet example. *The Tao* leads *Without* pressure. Likewise, we heal not by force but by *flow*. Influence comes from integrity, not intensity.

Reflection Questions

• Where are you trying to lead with control instead of *presence*?

• What does it look like to guide gently, *Without* force?

• How can you be the example today instead of giving advice?

Daily Affirmation

I lead by being, not by forcing.

Day / Chapter 58: Trust the Space

When leaders
are too
visible,
the people
grow
restless.

When leaders
are gentle,
the people
feel
free.

Misfortune
can hide
inside
a blessing.

Blessing
can rise
from
misfortune.

The Way
makes space
for all things
to
unfold.

Commentary

Sometimes, we don't need to fix or fill. We need to allow. In recovery, we learn to stop over-managing every detail. Peace comes from trust. *The Tao* reminds us that things change, balance returns, and grace *flows* when we stop grasping. Give *Life* room.

Reflection Questions

- Where are you filling space that needs to breathe?

- What would it look like to trust *Life* more today?

- How have your blessings come from past misfortunes?

Daily Affirmation

I make space for healing to unfold.

Day / Chapter 59: Discipline Is Nourishment

In leadership,
nothing is more
nourishing
than
restraint.

Discipline
Rooted in
stillness
endures.

Prepare
before
problems
arise.

Root yourself
early,
and your foundation
will grow
deep.

Commentary

Discipline doesn't have to be rigid. In recovery, discipline means returning to what *grounds* us: daily practices, quiet structure, and inner stillness. When we tend our *'Roots'* before storms come, we grow steady. *The Tao* doesn't demand control. It invites care.

Reflection Questions

• What does discipline mean to you in your recovery?

• How are your daily practices nourishing you?

• What can you do today to *Root* yourself deeper?

Daily Affirmation

I nourish myself through steady discipline.

Day / Chapter 60: Handle Life Gently

Govern a great nation
as you would cook
a small morsel
—gently.

The Way
does not fight
evil.

It lets it
burn out
on its own.

Those who
live
in The Way
are beyond
harm.

Their peace
protects
all things.

Commentary

In recovery, we stop overreacting. *The Tao* teaches us not to over-handle or overcorrect. Just as a small morsel falls apart with too much stirring, *Life* falls apart when we meddle. Now, we handle things gently with breath, with patience, and with trust.

Reflection Questions

• Where in your *life* are you stirring too much?

• How can you let things unfold more naturally, today?

• What does it look like to respond gently instead of reacting?

Daily Affirmation

I handle Life gently, and peace protects me.

Day / Chapter 61: Be the Lowland

A great nation
is like a lowland
—it draws all
rivers
to itself.

Weakness
overcomes strength
through
stillness.

By yielding,
it becomes
the stronger.

In stillness,
we lead.

Commentary

In recovery, we learn to lead not by dominance but by *presence*. *The Tao* reminds us that softness holds power. You don't need to be loud to be heard. You don't need to win to be strong. Be the lowland: open, *grounded*, receptive, and *Life flows* toward and through you.

Reflection Questions

- Where are you still trying to control or force?

- What would it look like to lead through stillness instead?

- How can you embrace your receptive nature today?

Daily Affirmation

I lead by grounding, not grasping.

Day / Chapter 62: The Treasure Within

The Way
is the
refuge
for all
things.

It's the
treasure
of the
good,
and the
protector
of the
broken.

Words may guide,
but presence
transforms.

Even the lost
can find
their way
in The Way.

Commentary

No matter where we've been, *The Tao* welcomes us back. Just like recovery, it holds space for the broken and the brave alike. You don't have to earn it. You only have to return. When we *live* from *The Tao*, even our silence becomes a gift to the world.

Reflection Questions

- When have you felt *The Tao* meet you in your brokenness?

- What does it mean to be treasured by something eternal?

- How can you extend that same grace to yourself today?

Daily Affirmation

The Way treasures even the lost.

Day / Chapter 63: Do the Simple Thing

Act
Without
doing.

Work
Without
forcing.

Find greatness
in the small.

Respond to difficulty
while it's
easy.

Big things
begin
small.

Hard things
begin
simple.

The Wise
handle all things
by letting them
unfold.

Commentary

Recovery is made of small, steady actions. We don't need to conquer the whole mountain. We just need to take the next step. *The Tao* teaches us that peace is simplicity. When we act *Without* pressure, we move in harmony. Start small. Stay steady. Let it build.

Reflection Questions

• What simple action can you take today toward healing?

• Where are you overcomplicating your recovery?

• What would it feel like to move with quiet steadiness?

Daily Affirmation

I do the simple things, and The Way unfolds.

Day / Chapter 64: Start Before It's Hard

What's at rest
is easy to
hold.

What's unformed
is easy to
shape.

Handle things
before they
harden.

Prevent trouble
before it
appears.

The tallest tree
grew from
the tiniest
seed.

Commentary

Recovery teaches us to listen early, before things spiral out of control. *The Tao* urges prevention, not reaction. Pay attention to small tensions, stray thoughts, and early signs of trouble. Don't wait for chaos to act. Be gentle and *present* now, and peace will take *Root*.

Reflection Questions

- Where in your *life* can you respond sooner and softer?

- What tension needs your attention before it becomes suffering?

- How can you stay *present* with what's just beginning to grow?

Daily Affirmation

I respond early and gently.

Day / Chapter 65: Wise Unknowing

The Wise ancients
did not teach
knowledge
—they taught
unknowing.

Trying to control
minds
leads to
cleverness.

Allowing space
leads to
harmony.

Empty minds.

Open hearts.

This is
true Wisdom.

Commentary

In recovery, we discover that trying to be clever got us nowhere. *'True Wisdom'* comes when we stop pretending to know. When we let go of being right, we become open. *The Tao flows* not through brilliance but through humility. Unknowing is the doorway to peace.

Reflection Questions

• Where can you practice unknowing today?

• How does letting go of 'figuring it out' bring you closer to *The Tao*?

• What does humble *Wisdom* feel like in your body and breath?

Daily Affirmation

I embrace unknowing and open to peace.

Day / Chapter 66: Lead From Below

The sea
is king of rivers
because it lies
lower than them.

The Wise lead
by placing themselves
last.

They serve,
and so are
trusted.

They do not
rise above.

They
fall into
place.

Commentary

Leadership in recovery is about humility. You don't need to stand above others to offer *Wisdom*. True strength comes from being real, accessible, and *grounded*. When we serve instead of control, we gain respect *Without* needing to demand it.

Reflection Questions

- Where are you still trying to be above or ahead?

- What does leadership through humility look like in your *life*?

- How can you serve others *Without* losing yourself?

Daily Affirmation

I lead by stepping back and serving.

Day / Chapter 67: The Three Treasures

I have
three treasures:

Compassion,
makes me
brave.

Simplicity,
makes me
generous.

Humility,
makes me
a leader.

Commentary

Recovery invites us to return to what matters. Not wealth. Not power. But heart. These three treasures of *The Tao:* compassion, simplicity, and humility, are the foundation of a *Life* in balance. They guide our relationships, our choices, and our growth.

Reflection Questions

- Which of these three treasures do you most need today?

- How do compassion and humility show up in your recovery?

- Where can you return to simplicity?

Daily Affirmation

I walk with compassion, simplicity, and humility.

Day / Chapter 68: The Best Warrior

The best
warrior
does not
dominate.

The best
fighter
does not
strike
in anger.

The best
winner
does not
compete.

This is
The Way:
to act
Without force,
to rise
Without pride.

Commentary

In addiction, aggression, anger, or the need to be right may have fueled us to need to win at all costs. Still, recovery shows us that real power is peaceful. *The Tao* teaches us to move *Without* force and to act *Without* ego. The strongest warrior is often the gentlest soul.

Reflection Questions

• Where are you still trying to win or prove something?

• What does peaceful strength feel like to you?

• How can you lead with gentleness today?

Daily Affirmation

My power is peaceful, not forceful.

Day / Chapter 69: The Strategy of Yielding

In conflict,
take a step
back.

Do not advance
unless
you must.

Hold your ground,
but never
provoke.

The greatest
victory
is found
through
peace.

Commentary

In recovery, we don't need to fight every battle. Sometimes, the wisest thing to do is to step back, breathe, and let things pass. *The Tao* reminds us that true strength lies in restraint. Peace is not weakness, it's *Wisdom* in motion.

Reflection Questions

- Where can you take a step back today instead of engaging?

- How does yielding make you stronger?

- What does it look like to seek peace instead of victory?

Daily Affirmation

I step back and allow peace to lead.

Day / Chapter 70: Few Will Understand

My words
are simple.

My Path
is clear
—yet few
will understand.

Those who
look deeply
will see.

The Way
is hidden,
but always
nearby.

Commentary

The Tao is not complicated. It's just subtle. Recovery can feel the same. We *live*, speak gently, act quietly, and still, some won't get it. That's okay. *The Tao* isn't for performance. It's for *presence*. Let your *path* be true, even if few follow.

Reflection Questions

- Where do you feel misunderstood on your recovery *path*?

- How do you stay true to your values, even when others don't understand?

- What does simplicity mean for you today?

Daily Affirmation

I walk The quiet Way Without needing approval.

Day / Chapter 71: Know Not Knowing

To know
you don't know
is
clarity.

To not know
you don't know
is
sickness.

The Wise
embrace
what they do not know
—and become
whole.

Commentary

In recovery, we learn that certainty can be a dangerous thing. It shuts doors. *The Tao* invites us to keep a 'beginner's mind.' Knowing that we don't know opens us to deeper insight, humility, and grace. Stay curious. Stay open. That is true *Wisdom.*

Reflection Questions

• Where do you pretend to know how to feel safe?

• How does embracing uncertainty bring you peace?

• What is one area where you could 'admit I don't know,' today?

Daily Affirmation

I am clear because I don't need to know.

Day / Chapter 72: Respect the Self

When people
lose respect,
they grow
numb.

Honor
begins
Within.

Don't chase
approval
—live with
dignity.

Let your
home
be
Within.

Commentary

Addiction often comes from abandoning ourselves. In recovery, we learn to respect our boundaries, needs, and values. *The Tao* reminds us that proper reverence begins *Within*. You don't need the world to see your worth. You only need to stop forgetting it.

Reflection Questions

- Where are you seeking approval that you no longer need?

- What does self-respect look like in your actions today?

- How can you make your inner world your safe home?

Daily Affirmation

I honor myself from Within Without.

Day / Chapter 73: Courage Without Force

Boldness
Without care
leads to
death.

Caution
Without courage
leads to
fear.

The Way
acts
Without striving
—yet
nothing is
left undone.

It trusts.

It waits.

It always
prevails.

Commentary

In recovery, we learn that forcing things backfires. So does hiding. *The Tao* teaches us courage that comes from calm, not ego. This is not recklessness. It's brave trust. The kind of courage that walks forward even when it's quiet inside.

Reflection Questions

• Where are you forcing instead of trusting?

• What would quiet courage look like today?

• How does faith change your response to fear?

Daily Affirmation

I move forward with trusting courage.

Day / Chapter 74: Let Life Lead

If you try
to take
Nature's place,
you'll lose
your way.

Only Life
holds
the power
of Life.

Let things
unfold.

Do not take
the seat
of judgment.

The Way
rules
Without control.

Commentary

We don't have to play God in recovery. We don't have to know the outcome or decide what others deserve. *The Tao* reveals that *Life* possesses its intelligence. When we stop interfering, peace has space to grow. Let go of the gavel. Let *Life* lead.

Reflection Questions

- Where are you trying to control what's not yours?

- How does judgment block your growth?

- What would it look like to trust the *Wisdom* of *Life* today?

Daily Affirmation

I let Life lead by releasing control.

Day / Chapter 75: The Cost of Excess

When leaders
hoard,
people suffer.

When desires
rule,
Life becomes
tight.

The Way
is simple
—enough
is enough.

The Wise
don't take
more than
they need.

Commentary

Addiction thrived in excess, too much of everything and never **enough**. Recovery is a return to simplicity. *The Tao* reminds us that satisfaction isn't about having more. It's about wanting less. In this case, *'enough'* is a serene word. It frees the soul.

Reflection Questions

• Where in your *life* do you still chase excess?

• What does *'enough'* feel like inside you?

• How can simplicity bring you back to *center*?

Daily Affirmation

I have enough. I am enough. I need nothing more.

Day / Chapter 76: Be Soft to Stay Alive

Alive,
we are soft
and flexible.

Dead,
we are hard
and stiff.

The hard
and proud
will break.

The soft
and yielding
endure.

The Way
favors
what bends.

Commentary

Rigidity often masks fear. In recovery, we soften so we can grow. *The Tao* tells us clearly what bends survive. What refuses breaks. Be open. Stay teachable. Flexibility is not a weakness, it's what keeps the heart *alive.*

Reflection Questions

• Where are you holding too tightly to your control or your opinion?

• What would it look like to soften just a little today?

• How has flexibility helped you heal?

Daily Affirmation

I stay alive by staying flexible.

Day / Chapter 77: Heaven's Bow

The Way
balances
Nature
—pulling down
the high,
lifting up
the low.

Taking from
excess,
giving to
lack.

The Way
does not
hoard.

It gives
freely
—like a bow
drawn smoothly.

Commentary

Recovery is about balance. Where we once took too much or gave too little, *The Tao* teaches reciprocity. When we find our *center*, we no longer hoard love, time, or energy. We become vessels of harmony, moving with the quiet rhythm of giving and receiving.

Reflection Questions

• Where is balance asking to be restored in your *life*?

• What are you hoarding out of fear?

• How can you let your *life* become a channel of *flow*?

Daily Affirmation

I give and receive balance Within The Way.

Day / Chapter 78: The Power of Water

Nothing
is softer
than water.

Yet nothing
is stronger
at wearing down
stone.

It flows
around
all resistance.

It prevails
by
yielding.

This is
The Way
of The Way.

Commentary

Water doesn't force. It *flows*. Recovery invites us to do the same. We become powerful not by pushing but by persisting. Gentleness is our strength. The more we trust the *flow*, the less we fear the obstacles. Like water, we find our *way*.

Reflection Questions

- Where can you stop pushing and start *flowing*?

- How has gentleness moved mountains in your recovery?

- What would it mean to follow *The Way* of water today?

Daily Affirmation

I flow like water: gentle, strong, and clear.

Day / Chapter 79: Beyond Scorekeeping

Even after
a truce,
resentment
may remain.

The Way
asks us
to let go.

The Wise
keep no score,
demand no repayment.

They live
in harmony,
not in
comparison.

Commentary

Scorekeeping kills peace. In recovery, we stop keeping track of every hurt, every debt. We forgive, not to forget, but to be free. *The Tao* reminds us that proper balance doesn't come from counting. It comes from letting go. Let go of the ledger. Let *Life flow* again.

Reflection Questions

• Who or what are you keeping score with?

• What would forgiveness feel like, even if not asked for?

• How can you *live* in balance, not comparison?

Daily Affirmation

I release the score and live in harmony.

Day / Chapter 80: Small and Simple

Let the village
be small,
the people
few.

Let them return
to simple
ways.

Let them find joy
in home and heart
—not conquest
or glory.

In stillness,
they are
whole.

Commentary

You don't need to *live* big to *live* fully. Recovery teaches us to find joy in the quiet, warm food, a safe space, and a clear mind. *The Tao* values the humble, the slow, and the real. Keep your world small, and your peace will grow large.

Reflection Questions

- Where have you confused success with noise or scale?

- What small joy is calling for your attention today?

- How can simplicity help you recover what matters?

Daily Affirmation

In simplicity, I find joy.

Day / Chapter 81: The Last Word

True words
aren't
fancy.

Fancy words
aren't
true.

The Wise
don't argue.

Those who have
don't boast.

Those who live
The Way
don't cling.

The Way gives
—and keeps
Without.

Commentary

This final chapter from *The Tao* is a mirror: simple, humble, and generous. Recovery invites us to stop clinging and to be kind, quiet, and clear. *Wisdom* doesn't argue. Love doesn't show off. *The Tao* gives freely, and so can we. This is the last word, and it is *'enough.'*

Reflection Questions

• What final lesson are you holding from this journey?

• How can you embody kindness *Without* needing recognition?

• What are you ready to release now so something new can begin?

Daily Affirmation

I give, release, and begin again.

Final Blessing

May The quiet Way
continue to guide your steps
—not with force,
but with flow.

Not with fear,
but with presence.

You have walked through shadow
and returned to light
—not as someone new,
but as someone true.

Let the Wisdom of The Way
become the rhythm of your days.

Let surrender be your strength,
and stillness your sanctuary.

The Way does not end,
and neither does your becoming.

Wherever you are,
whatever you carry,
however the winds may change
—remember:

You are not alone.
You are not broken.
You are already walking The Way.

Go,
gently.
Freely.

Without!

With love,

Miguel J. Rios

About the Author & Next Steps

Miguel J. Rios is a writer, educator, recovery advocate, and creative guide whose work bridges ancient *Taoist Wisdom* with modern healing practices. After navigating his own path through addiction, Miguel began exploring mindfulness, presence, and paradox as vehicles for spiritual renewal. His writings, poetic, reflective, and fiercely gentle, invite readers to reclaim their stillness and walk *The Way* back to themselves.

Miguel lives in New York, where he continues to write, teach, design, and facilitate conversations *Rooted* in compassion and clarity.

Continue the Journey

Would you like to deepen your practice or share this book with others?

• *The Way Within Without Recovery Edition* **Workbook:**

> **All new!** Daily journaling prompts expanded self-inquiry and reflection space to walk *The Way* at your own rhythm.

• *The Way Within Without Recovery Edition* **Facilitator's Guide:**
> Designed for group recovery circles, offering weekly reflection scripts, discussion questions, and thematic guidance.

➤ Available at:

www.thewaywithinwithout.com

For updates, digital downloads, or facilitation support, visit the website or connect directly at:

miguel@thewaywithinwithout.com

www.ingramcontent.com/pod-product-compliance
Lightning Source LLC
Chambersburg PA
CBHW070919130626
46555CB00001B/206